How **Wachou** Became **King**

Joanne Zintel

Illustrated by Dwight Nacaytuna

To order additional copies of this book, contact:
Xlibris
1-888-795-4274
www.Xlibris.com
Orders@Xlibris.com

ISBN: Softcover   978-1-7960-5333-3
        EBook   978-1-7960-5332-6

Print information available on the last page

Rev. date: 08/16/2019

<u>Dedicated to:</u>

All of the Bilingual Resource Teachers in the Madison Public Schools, Madison, Wisconsin, and the Families and Especially the Children who were enriched by their dedication and love of culture, language and teaching.

Once upon a time there was a boy named Wachou. He wanted to be the King of all the people. He went up to the high mountain and he asked the Spirit One, "Can I be King of all the people?" The Spirit One answered, "Not yet, Wachou. Not Yet. First you must do a very great thing."

So Wachou went to school and got A+ in everything. He spoke many languages. Again he went up the high mountain and asked the Spirit One, "Now can I be King of all the people?" The Spirit One answered, "Not yet, Wachou. Not yet. First you must do a very great thing."

So Wachou worked for his family growing food for all the people in the village. He met a very smart and beautiful girl named Pang. Soon they were married and had a son. Then Wachou went up the high mountain and asked the Spirit One, "Now can I be King of all the people?" Again the Spirit One answered, "Not yet, Wachou. Not yet. First you must do a very great thing."

Then the war began and Wachou became a soldier. He was very brave and had to leave his family for a while to help save the good people in his country. Then he returned to his own village to save his own family. They had to cross the Great River to be safe from the evil people. When he felt safe he once again went up the high mountain and asked the Spirit One, "Now can I be King of all the people?" But the Spirit One answered, "Not yet, Wachou. Not yet. First you must do a very great thing."

Wachou started to learn English and after two years he traveled far from his own country to a new land called America. He helped his family in this new land and soon they began to understand the language and make their home in this new land. Once again Wachou went up to the high mountain and asked the Spirit One, "Now can I be King of all the people?" But, again, the Spirit One answered, "Not yet, Wachou. Not yet. First you must do a very great thing."

Wachou wanted to do this very great thing. But what was it that the Spirit One wanted him to do? He decided to start a store so he could sell food that his own people would like and food they knew how to cook. He worked long hours carrying rice to his store and traveling to other cities to buy food for his store. He helped his son with his homework, especially his math. And he spent long hours talking quietly to his wife about the land that they had left and about his dream to be king of all the people. Once again he went up to the high mountain and asked the Spirit One, "Now can I be King of all the people?" But the Spirit one once again answered, "Not yet, Wachou. Not yet. First you must do a very great thing."

One day Wachou's brother came to him and said, "I'm worried about our peoples' children. They are forgetting the land we left and our ways. They need someone to help them understand where they come from. They need someone to teach them to be proud of their culture and their language and the ways of their parents and grandparents. Who can help our children?"

Wachou listened to his brother. He knew what his brother was saying was true. He thought and thought about this problem. And then he knew what he had to do. HE HAD TO BECOME A TEACHER! He had to help teach the children about the old ways in the country they had left. He had to help teach the children about the new ways in their new land. He had to help teach them how to go from one culture to another. And he had to help the parents understand their children so that everyone could live in peace and be proud and happy.

He began to teach the children. He taught them for many years. He taught Lewis and Tony and Mytry and Gordie. He taught Jason and Jay and Jenny and Narry. He taught many, many children and they learned the old ways of the country they had left. They began to value the language and culture of their parents. And they learned the new ways of their new country. Wachou helped them realize that being bilingual was beautiful and they were proud and happy. And their parents and grandparents were proud of them and they too were happy.

Then Wachou went up the high mountain and asked the Spirit One, "Now can I be King of all the people?" The Spirit One smiled at him and said, "Wachou, now you are ready. You have done a very great thing teaching our children. You can now be King of all the people." And he gave Wachou the power to be a very good King. And Wachou and his family and his people lived a very long time and were very happy.

The End

Printed in the United States
By Bookmasters